CAREERS IN

DESIGN AND PROTOTYPING

CARLA MOONEY

Rosen YA

New York

Published in 2020 by The Rosen Publishing Group, Inc.
29 East 21st Street, New York, NY 10010

First Edition

Library of Congress Cataloging-in-Publication Data

Names: Mooney, Carla, 1970– author.
Title: Careers in design and prototyping / Carla Mooney.
Description: First edition. | New York : Rosen Publishing, 2020. | Series: Makerspace careers | Audience: Grades 7–12. | Includes bibliographical references and index.
Identifiers: LCCN 2018047079 | ISBN 9781508187981 (library bound) | ISBN 9781508187974 (pbk.)
Subjects: LCSH: Industrial design—Vocational guidance—Juvenile literature. | Makerspaces—Juvenile literature.
Classification: LCC TS171 .M653 2020 | DDC 745.2—dc23
LC record available at https://lccn.loc.gov/2018047079

Manufactured in China

CONTENTS

INTRODUCTION

When Jack Wesson's girlfriend could not visit her family over fall break, the Yale University student took her to the school's art and technology makerspace, the Center for Collaborative Arts & Media (CCAM). At the makerspace, his girlfriend put on a headset and was virtually transported to her hometown of Malibu, California. Using a Google Earth virtual-reality experience, she took Wesson on a tour of her childhood neighborhood.

Reopened in 2017 after a renovation, Yale's CCAM is a place where people from various fields can collaborate on projects and use a wide range of media resources, including cutting-edge digital tools. Numerous artists and experts in dance, drama, music, the visual arts, and computer science support the center and guide students. "One of the center's virtues is that it brings together all of these really talented and innovative people into a single space," said Johannes DeYoung, the center's director and senior critic at Yale School of Art in a 2018 article posted on Yale's website. "People bump into each other here and something really interesting and unique can serendipitously emerge from it. Where else does that happen?"

At the CCAM, students can reserve creative suites to work with a variety of equipment, including drawing tablets, mixers and editing instruments, XR (extended-reality)

Students gather around a computer and watch as a woman wearing a virtual-reality headset tests the design of a new computer-generated simulction.

production tools, and more. As a junior majoring in computer science and art, Wesson spends a lot of time at the makerspace. He takes several classes there, works on an independent study project, and helps others use the center's resources. Because Wesson plans to pursue a career in virtual reality, the time he spends at the technology makerspace gives him hands-on learning experiences that will help him in his future career. "The center is invaluable to me," he said. "I actually can't imagine my life right now without it."

Makerspaces like Yale's CCAM are springing up in communities across the country. At a makerspace, people can come together to work on projects and share ideas, equipment, and expertise. Makerspaces can take many forms. They can be located in schools and libraries or be a stand-alone facility. These spaces give community members access to equipment such as 3D printers, laser cutters, soldering irons, sewing machines, milling and machining tools, and more. Low-tech supplies like cardboard, wood, plastic, metal, and batteries are often available for creating art or prototyping ideas. In makerspaces with computers, users can experiment and learn how to use computer-aided design and graphic design software. At makerspaces, students, makers, and entrepreneurs can collaborate with others and share knowledge.

Makerspaces have also become a place where entrepreneurs can work to develop a product and build a design prototype. Tom Panzarella is the chief executive officer of Love Park Robotics, a startup company that works out of a makerspace called NextFab Studio in Philadelphia. He believes the space makes his company get taken more seriously. "You're not these two guys in a garage building a robot, right? You have your 21,000-square-foot [1,950-square-meter] production space; the boardroom here is really nice if we need to have meetings," he said in a 2014 article on NPR.org. "We look a lot more established than we really are." At NextFab, members like Panzarella have access to expensive tools such as high-end laser cutters and 3D printers. Members also benefit from the skills and experiences of each other. Panzarella was able to hire a mechanical engineer at NextFab to help him attach a video camera to his wheelchairs. "So, we effectively contract out to him some of our mechanical work, and it's like we have a mechanical engineer on staff," Panzarella said.

At makerspaces, students participate in hands-on learning, develop critical-thinking skills, and gain confidence. They learn essential skills in science, technology, engineering, math, and the arts. In a makerspace, students will find countless opportunities to try out new technology.

CHAPTER ONE

USING MAKERSPACES FOR DESIGN AND PROTOTYPING

At Penn State Erie, the Behrend College, engineering students are actively learning about the design and prototyping process. Because of a grant from the Schreyer Institute for Teaching Excellence, Professor Charlotte de Vries has set up a makerspace where students in her Introduction to Engineering Design course can design robots and build prototypes of their designs. "I think prototyping is very important for students because there's a lot that works when you say, 'This is what I'm going to do,' and then actually trying to make it you are going to find a lot more hiccups," she said in a 2018 article on the Penn State website. In the course, students use special hardware and software to design their robots. Then they build prototypes, starting with the chassis or base frame. They add initial prototyping materials, such as cardboard, Popsicle sticks, and zip ties, to build the prototype. They use this prototype to assess the design's reliability and appearance. They also

A teacher guides students and gives feedback as they practice design and prototyping skills while building a robotic vehicle.

use the prototype to identify any bugs in the robot's design. After making any necessary design changes, students create a more sophisticated prototype using tools such as laser cutters and 3D printers. This prototype more closely resembles the final product both in how it looks and functions.

Professor de Vries's students have created a variety of designs and prototypes, such as a miniature aircraft designed to look like the spaceship in the movie *Guardians of the Galaxy*. Another student created a prototype of a robotic car shaped like a pizza slice that could carry pizza from one point to another. Students agreed that working on their projects helped them better understand the actual process of designing a product. In an article on the Penn State website, student Erin Loc said the project changed how she thought about design and engineering. "I began thinking of engineering as problem solving rather than just simply building things."

WHAT IS THE DESIGN PROCESS?

A new product does not just appear from thin air. A person—or often a team of people—work to create it. Long before a product hits store shelves, designers are working on it through the design process. The design process has several steps. At its core, design is a way to solve a problem. Therefore, before any design work can begin, the first step of the design process is to understand exactly what the problem is. Designers spend a lot of time researching a problem and gathering facts to answer the following questions:

> What is the problem or need?
> Whom does the problem affect?
> Why is the problem important to solve?

Once they have defined the problem, designers think about what needs to be included in a solution. They develop design requirements, which are the important characteristics a solution must have in order to be successful. Design requirements are something that is necessary to solve the design problem. Design requirements include details such as size, cost, materials, functionality, and ease of use.

After design requirements are set, designers generate product ideas to solve the design problem. Often, they try to brainstorm as many solutions as they can before picking the best one. Even an idea that seems crazy at first might have some features that make another idea better. Once designers come up with a list of possible ideas, they pick the best one (or ones) to develop. They look at each possible solution and see how it meets the design requirements. In addition to design requirements, some features are nice to have. Ideas that include some desirable, but not required, features might be better than others. Designers also consider other factors, such as time and cost to make it, robustness, aesthetic appeal, or the skills needed to make the product. Designers consider all of this information to decide which design idea is the best.

Once the designers have picked an idea, development begins. Designs can be developed in several ways. One of the most common techniques is sketching. Sketching quickly puts an idea into a visual format that everyone can easily see. Designers use several types of sketches and drawings, which progress to become increasingly refined and include details about the product's appearance, proportions, scale, layouts, and more. Some drawings are photo-like representations of a design. Other drawings are more technical and show a product's actual size and shape and how its parts work together.

Once the idea has been developed, designers create a model. Creating a model helps designers identify areas of the design that need to be adjusted. Some models are physical objects. A scale model is a copy of an object that is usually smaller than the actual size of the object. Other models are full-size, 3D models. They can be made of

This designer uses plastic pieces created by a 3D printer to build a design model. With a 3D model, designers can more easily identify design flaws and make necessary adjustments.

materials such as cardboard or Styrofoam or created by 3D printers. Other virtual models are generated by a computer. The next step in the design process is to create a pro-

totype. A prototype is a working version of a product. Building a prototype allows the designers to test the structure, function, and appearance of the product. A prototype can be built with different materials from the final product. It is often not as polished as the final product.

Testing and redesign are some of the most important steps in the design process. Designers use prototypes to test how a product will work. Users interact with the prototype and give designers feedback about how the product works, what they like about it, and what needs improvement. With this information, designers make changes to the design to make the product better. The testing process often involves multiple loops, with more testing of the redesigned product. Although the process can be tedious, testing and redesign make a design the best it can be.

FIND A MAKERSPACE

Makerspaces can be found in communities across the country. Students interested in exploring and learning at a makerspace can see if there is one located at their school, local library, or community center. In addition, students can search several online directories to find makerspaces in their local area. These include:

Makerspace.com
MakerDirectory.com
The Maker Map
NexPBC

Many makerspaces offer a variety of programs, workshops, classes, and meetings for community members. In these spaces, students can take classes in computer-aided design, mold making, circuit making, 3D printing, programming, metalworking, screen printing, woodworking, and more.

DESIGNING IN A MAKERSPACE

Makerspaces are ideal places to work through the design process. Students, entrepreneurs, and other makers can use makerspaces to share resources and knowledge. Once they have identified a problem and brainstormed a solution, makers can use a makerspace's computer technology to

In a school makerspace, a student can learn design skills. This student uses a 3D printer to create a 3D plastic model.

create digital designs and sketches. They can use supplies such as cardboard, wood, plastic and metal pieces, and batteries to build prototypes. They can also learn how to use technologies and tools such as 3D printers, laser cutters, woodworking tools, and more to create models and prototypes.

In 2010, Apple unveiled the first iPad. A few months later, entrepreneur Patrick Buckley had an idea. Many of his friends and family did not want to use an iPad to read because they loved the feel of a physical book. To solve the problem, Buckley came up with an idea to create a product that made an iPad feel like sitting down with a book. Yet like many entrepreneurs, Buckley did not have the tools at home to develop and build his design. He also did not have the money to pay a design company to do it for him. Instead, Buckley turned to TechShop, a chain of workshop-like makerspaces that had all of the high-tech and heavy-duty equipment that he needed. In four weeks, Buckley designed and built a prototype for a bamboo-and-moleskin iPad holder that made the tablet feel more like holding a book. He called his product the DODOcase. It quickly became a hit with tech-savvy customers. Buckley sold $1 million-worth of DODOcases in the first four months after the iPad's release. Today, the DODOcase company creates a variety of stylish cases and sleeves for tablets, phones, and other portable technology. Buckley credits the TechShop maker-space with giving him the tools to get started. "I don't know what I would have done if TechShop didn't exist," he said in a 2011 article on Newsweek.com.

CHAPTER TWO

PRODUCT DESIGN

Since the dawn of humanity, people have searched for better solutions to specific problems. They tried to make better tools, weapons, and more. When creating each new item, they thought hard about it—what problem are they trying to solve, what are they trying to accomplish, how can they make it work better? By answering these questions, they created a product design.

WHAT IS PRODUCT DESIGN?

Product design is the entire process of creating usable products and experiences. It includes defining real-world problems and brainstorming possible solutions. Product design also includes planning every aspect of a product before it is made, including making decisions about how a

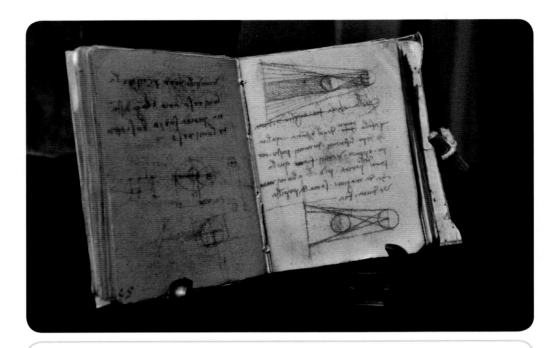

The codex of Leonardo da Vinci is a collection of scientific writings by the Italian inventor and artist. In his notebooks, Leonardo often sketched designs for his inventions.

product is used, what technologies it uses, the materials it is made from, and how it looks and feels. And perhaps most importantly, design is creating a product that solves a problem and works as intended. In the words of Apple Inc.'s late CEO Steve Jobs, "Design is not just what it looks and feels like. Design is how it works."

At the same time, design is much more than creating a product that works. If a fitness band works but is difficult to use, people will not want to buy it again. In this way, design is creating a product that people want to use. If the design of a fitness band isn't quite right and users feel uncomfortable or frustrated every time they use it, they probably won't buy that model again. They might even tell their friends not to buy it. Good product design balances form with function every time. Good design combines the right materials, colors, details, and form to make users want to buy and use a product.

Good product design can have a dramatic impact on everyday life, changing how people live and work. For example, the smartphone is an example of an innovative product design that has changed the way people communicate, get information, listen to music, and more. There are examples of product design everywhere. The tablet computer in a student's backpack, the clock on the wall, the microwave in the kitchen, and the chair at a desk are all created by product design. Everything manmade that can be seen and touched was designed by someone.

WORKING IN PRODUCT DESIGN

Product designers invent new products or make existing ones better. They work in a wide range of industries. They combine art, business, and engineering to design products that people use daily. In every design, they consider a product's function, costs, usability, and aesthetics. In their designs, product designers also consider both the materials that will be used in a product and how it will be made or manufactured.

Product designers typically work as part of a team, which includes market researchers, designers, engineers, marketing experts, and more. They may be part of a company's in-house design team, or they may work for a consulting company that is hired to help clients with product design. Together, the team defines and understands the problem that they are trying to solve with design. Then they will work through the design process.

As part of the design process, a designer meets with clients or users to determine the requirements for a design, including what problem it will solve and what functions it needs to include. The designers gather information and research the ways a product might be used and who will use it. They sketch designs, both by hand and using computer-aided design (CAD) software to create 2D and 3D visuals of the design. They can also use CAD software to develop virtual models of the design that the team can review and use to identify areas in the design that need to be adjusted.

Often, the designer will create a physical prototype of the product. A prototype is a working version of a product. It allows the design team to develop and test the structure, function, and appearance of the product. Sometimes, the design team will make several prototypes during the design process until the design is just right.

A designer sketches ideas for new products at the French company Babymoov, which creates everyday products to simplify life for parents and children.

Connor Macmillan is a product designer for Dyson, a British company that designs and manufactures household appliances such as vacuum cleaners, hair dryers, and blade-less fans. In his role, he develops new features for Dyson's digital-connected products. He said in a 2018 article on the Jobsite website:

> I work on everything from research and innova-
> tion, to driving those designs into the delivery
> stage. The day could start with initial concepts
> on Post-It notes generating new ideas as if in the
> mindset of your users. By collaborating with peers,
> we can quickly assess which ideas are best before
> developing them in more detail using software or
> 3D model making skills.

One of the challenges Macmillan faces as a designer is making sure his design meets the user's needs and wants. "The best way for me to overcome the challenge is to build something physical or digital that I get into peoples' hands to then gain feedback on. With this feedback, I can improve the design and re-test it. By doing this repeatedly, I try to iron out all the little faults and produce something great," he said.

HOW TO BECOME A PRODUCT DESIGNER

For those interested in creating and building in maker-spaces, the career field of product design is a natural fit. Most product design jobs require a bachelor's degree in

A product designer sketches a pencil drawing of a new product idea to convey his vision of the design to others on the design team.

industrial design, engineering, architecture, or a related field from a four-year college or university. Many programs require students to take classes in drawing, computer-aided design (CAD), and 3D modeling, along with classes in industrial materials and processes, manufacturing methods, and business.

People interested in product design should also have strong artistic and design skills. Before a student is admitted to a product design bachelor's degree

STANDX

In 2011, Simon Hong's own experience with back pain led him to conceive an idea to help users who sat for many hours in front of a computer. A neuroscience researcher at the Massachusetts Institute of Technology (MIT), Hong designed the StandX, a robotic chair that nudged users to shift positions every few minutes. He first built a prototype of StandX in 2011 and applied for a patent. The chair's seat is split down the middle and each half can be parallel or perpendicular to the ground. Users can set a timer on the chair that gently vibrates to remind the user to switch into a different position every few minutes. While working full-time at MIT, Hong worked nights and weekends to build fifteen early models of StandX at Artisan's Asylum, a local makerspace in Somerville, Massachusetts, that had the equipment he needed. "Each chair took about one month to build," Hong said in a 2018 article in the *Boston Globe*. "After I finished my daily work at MIT, I would have dinner at home, and then go to Artisan's Asylum." Hong often worked on his chairs until 2 or 3 a.m. Hong has also set up a company, Robilis, and hired an interim CEO. "Sitting long hours is pretty bad," Hong said in the *Boston Globe* article. "When the product is out, I think it will catch on pretty soon."

program, some schools may require students to complete basic art and design courses and submit sketches and other art samples. Many programs help students build a professional portfolio of their designs, which they can use to demonstrate design skills when applying for a job.

People in product design should also have strong computer skills. Computers are frequently used by designers. They use computer-aided design (CAD) and computer-aided drafting and design (CADD) software to sketch ideas and create 3D models. "Learn prototyping software like Solidworks or Adobe Illustrator so you can quickly draw up your ideas," advises Macmillan in the 2018 Jobsite article. "Workshop, model-making and 3D rapid prototyping skills will quickly turn 2D into 3D to understand the context of your ideas."

Even without a degree in a design field, those interested in product design can build their skills and demonstrate proficiency by getting experience. Some students work in a design internship for a company or design firm. Students can also gain experience by taking art and design classes or camps. Using makerspaces, they can even practice the design process, coming up with a problem to solve, designing a solution, and building a prototype.

JOB OUTLOOK

According to the Bureau of Labor Statistics, employment of industrial designers, which includes product designers, is expected to grow between 2016 and 2026 by 4 percent. This rate of growth is slightly lower than the average growth rate of all occupations (7 percent). Other potential careers in product design include UX (user-experience) design, industrial design, prototype technician, and more.

A young designer uses a computer-aided design program as he collaborates with the design team and works remotely on his laptop.

The public's demand for innovative products and new product styles continues to create demand for designers. In addition, as the demand for new technologies and digital products grows, designers with a high degree of technical ability and design sophistication will be in greater demand. Candidates with strong computer skills and experience in computer-aided design (CAD) and related software programs will have the best prospects for landing a good job in product design. In addition, as more products become internet connected and digital, candidates who have experience working with user interfaces and interactive design will be in demand.

CHAPTER THREE

COMPUTER-AIDED DESIGN

Today, many product designers use specialized computer software to explore design ideas. Computer-aided design (CAD) software allows designers to create sketches and models on a computer, making the design process faster and more efficient than ever before. For all types of products, CAD software allows designers to explore ideas, visualize designs, create virtual models, and produce them.

CAD software can perform many complex tasks. Designers use these programs to design a product and document the design process. With CAD software, designers can produce 2D drawings or 3D models that can be rotated and viewed from any angle. They look almost exactly like the finished product. Two-dimensional flat drawings show a product's overall dimensions, such as its height, length, and width. Three-dimensional CAD virtual models show more detail about each individual component of the product. In addition to showing its size

A designer uses a computer-aided design program to create a virtual model of each component that will be used in a new product.

and shape, 3D CAD models show how the components fit and work together.

Using CAD speeds up the design process. When designers need to make a change, they do not have to redraw entire designs. Instead, they can use the CAD digital file and make the necessary changes, while keeping the rest of the design the same. When the design is finished, CAD software produces electronic files for manufacturing or machining. The files also include information about materials, processes, dimensions, and more.

CAD software also allows designers to analyze a design through simulations. A simulation creates a virtual environment that looks, feels, and behaves like the real world to test a design. Designers can use a simulation to test their model to see how it reacts to heat, pressure, physical forces, and other conditions. In a simulation, designers can determine the strengths and weaknesses of their design without building a physical prototype. This saves a lot of time and money in the design process.

WORKING IN COMPUTER-AIDED DESIGN

People with an interest in design and computer science may find a career in CAD to be a good fit. There are several careers that rely on computer-aided design. Industrial designers create the designs for manufactured products, such as cars, appliances, and toys. They combine art and technology to develop products that are both functional and attractive. Industrial designers use CAD software to sketch ideas and create 3D virtual models of their ideas. They consult with engineers and other production and manufacturing professionals on the design. Then they create prototypes that users can test and evaluate. Often, industrial designers specialize in a particular type of product, such as toys or appliances.

Many engineering jobs also use computer-aided design to create tools, engines, machines, and electrical equipment. Electrical and electronic engineers and technicians design and develop computers, communications equipment, medical devices, navigation equipment, and other electronics. Mechanical engineers and technicians design, develop, and test mechanical devices, such as tools, engines, and machines.

CAD technicians, also known as CAD drafters or CAD operators, use CAD software to take the designs of architects or engineers and produce detailed, technical, and interactive drawings of many objects, from computer chips to buildings. CAD technicians work from rough sketches created by designers, engineers, or architects. Using CAD software, they create and store digital versions of the drawings that contain information on how to build an object or structure, its dimensions, and the materials needed to complete the project. CAD technicians create schematics for a project that can be viewed, printed, or programmed directly into other systems, such as building information modeling (BIM) systems used in the construction industry. Using digital files, CAD technicians and other members of the project team can create and collaborate on digital models of the structure or object. They can also see how different parts of the project work together.

At Displayplan, tech designers work on projects to create in-store display programs for leading brands and retailers. For example, the company designed a flat-pack display box for Mars chocolate that created an appealing display of several candy bars. For each project, the company's concept team brainstorms ideas and creates visuals to share with clients. Then, the technical team takes over to bring the idea to life and develop a production-ready design. In an interview posted on the Displayplan website, one of the company's tech designers described the typical process:

The majority of our work is done in SolidWorks [a type of CAD software] but I still opt for the trusty pen and paper at the beginning of a project, taking the time to think through the best way of approaching a problem. After quickly sketching ideas, the process moves into CAD modeling, where we can get a real sense for the best way to mass-produce a design.

After the design has been developed in CAD software, the tech designer creates quick prototypes for testing. They use 3D printers and a fully stocked workshop with traditional machinery and a laser cutter. The tech designer described the next steps:

The process of testing physical prototypes prior to the manufacturing stage of a project is something we believe strongly in. We prototype every design we create, either through fabricators, or our workshop staff. We typically then use these prototypes to show our clients how a project has progressed through the technical design stage from the first visuals our concept team created.

At the end of this process, the design is ready for production.

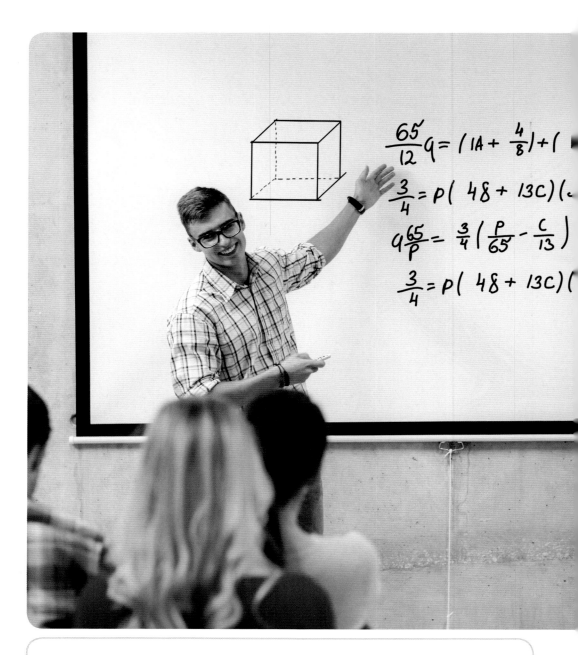

$$\frac{65}{12}q = (1A + \frac{4}{8}) + ($$

$$\frac{3}{4} = p(48 + 13C)($$

$$q\frac{65}{p} = \frac{3}{4}\left(\frac{p}{65} - \frac{c}{13}\right)$$

$$\frac{3}{4} = p(48 + 13C)($$

A design student stands in front of the teacher and class to explain and solve several mathematical equations written on a whiteboard.

HOW TO GET A JOB IN COMPUTER-AIDED DESIGN

The requirements to land a job in computer-aided design vary by company and position. Positions as drafters, CAD operators, CAD technicians, and engineering technicians often require a two-year associate's degree from a technical institute or community college. These programs include courses in design fundamentals, sketching, and CAD software. To prepare for these programs, high school students should take classes in math, science, computer technology, graphic design, programming, and if available, drafting. In addition, many makerspaces offer classes and workshops in CAD, in which students can get experience using the software.

For those interested in careers in engineering, most positions require candidates to have at least a bachelor's degree from a four-year college or university. Students may choose to major in a specific engineering field, such as electronics, electrical, mechanical, or similar fields. These programs

CORD BUDDY

As an information technology professional, Steve Kwak was frustrated when his cell phone charging cord constantly fell to the floor behind his dresser. One night in 2005, he decided to design a solution. He started designing the Cord Buddy with sketches on paper. Then, he began using a software drawing program called Paint. "I was trying to create a unique method for securing the cord—one that would allow me to build different forms and exterior designs around the same functional method," he said in a profile of his product included in *Makers Who Made It: 100 Stories of Starting a Business*. Kwak gathered supplies at hardware, hobby, and craft stores to build his prototype. He worked at night and on weekends learning how to sew materials together, saw wood, form steel and aluminum, and work with other materials. With each prototype, he had family members test it and give feedback. "Once I selected a design, I sent my drawing directly to my chosen manufacturer partner and had them put the drawings into a professional CAD program to my specifications. Once I approved, they then created the official prototypes." In 2013, Kwak launched the Cord Buddy.

include classroom work, laboratory work, and field studies. Students take courses in mathematics, life and physical sciences, engineering, design, electrical circuits, and more. Many engineering programs also encourage students to work in an internship to gain valuable hands-on experience and apply the skills they have learned in the classroom to real-world designs.

Those interested in industrial design careers typically earn a bachelor's degree in industrial design, architecture, or engineering. Most programs include courses in graphic design, computer-aided design, sketching, drawing, 3D rendering, and other computer programs. Math and physical science courses are also good to take. No matter what level of education they have, students interested in CAD careers should build a portfolio of work that they can use to demonstrate their CAD skills for potential employers.

Some CAD professionals choose to earn a certification to show they have the skills for the job. For example, the American Design Drafting Association (ADDA) offers a professional certification for CAD technicians. In order to become certified, candidates must complete coursework and pass an examination.

An engineering student uses a soldering iron on an electronic board prototype after creating the initial design in a CAD program.

JOB OUTLOOK

The job outlook for CAD careers is good. According to the Bureau of Labor Statistics, jobs for drafters, which includes CAD operators, are projected to grow 7 percent from 2016 to 2026. This rate of growth is about the average of all occupations. Other CAD careers are also projected for strong growth from 2016 to 2026, including electrical and electronics engineers (7 percent), industrial designers (4 percent), mechanical engineering technicians (5 percent), and mechanical engineers (9 percent). The growth in these careers is primarily being driven by growth in the engineering services and construction industries. As long as these industries continue to grow, the need for engineers in this field will continue to grow as well.

Candidates with experience and skills in the latest software tools, especially those with CAD skills and the ability to create virtual simulations, will be in high demand because these skills allow companies to reduce the time and cost of the product development cycle.

CHAPTER FOUR

DESIGN AND ELECTRONICS

E very year, new, high-tech devices are unveiled at consumer electronics shows. From laptops and tablets to smartphones and televisions, today's high-end electronics incorporate cutting-edge engineering and design solutions. The life cycle of these products is short, with new products constantly being introduced to the market. A few months after the unveiling of a new design, the hardware and software are outdated, the design is stale and something else has become the new must-have gadget.

THE ELECTRONICS INDUSTRY

The electronics industry creates the new technology that consumers use now and in the future. Semiconductor companies design chips or integrated circuits. An integrated circuit is a set of electronic circuits set on a single piece

A woman holds a smartphone with several icons on its screen. Electronics product designers create the latest electronic gadgets consumers want to use.

of semiconductor material, such as silicon. Other companies design electrical components, such as resistors and capacitors. Consumer electronics companies take the chips and other components and use them in the design of electronic products like washing machines, microwaves, smartphones, fitness trackers, and more.

The electronics industry is constantly evolving and changing as new products and technologies are developed. According to the Electrical and Electronic Manufacturing Market Briefing 2017, the global market for electrical and electronics manufacturing is expected to reach $3 trillion by 2020. With so much demand for new electronic devices, there are a lot of opportunities for the people who design and create these products.

WORKING IN ELECTRONICS DESIGN

For those with an interest in design and high-tech electronics, a career in electronics design may be appealing. Electronics designers create and develop electronic components, software, products, or systems for a variety of uses. Some work to design computer hardware. Others, called circuit designers, create designs for electronic circuits and circuit boards.

Electronics designers begin each new project by defining what the new electronic device should be able to do. They use computers to design the circuits and other parts of the electronics for the project. They design how electrical power is used to operate a device or improve how it works. Once they have completed the design, the electronics designer will build a prototype for testing. Testing helps the design team identify any problems in the prototype and adjust the design to fix the problem and improve the product.

In 2009, Jim McKelvey, a computer engineer and glass blower, had the sale of one of his $2,000 glass faucets fall through because he could

not accept the customer's credit card. Frustrated, he got together with his friends Jack Dorsey and Tristan O'Tierney, an iOS engineer, to design a new electronic device

A customer swipes a credit card through a Square card reader attached to the vendor's mobile phone to easily make a payment.

that would allow individuals and small business owners to accept mobile payments. "I knew what it was like to be a small merchant and be excluded from commerce because I didn't have a credit card system," said McKelvey in an Inc.com article. They built a prototype and took it to major banks and credit card companies for a demonstration. In 2009, they launched their company, Square, Inc. In 2010, Square launched their first product, the Card Reader, a 1-inch-square (6.5-centimeters-square) white device that plugs into the headphone jack of a smartphone or tablet and turns it into a credit card processor. Today, millions of merchants use the Square Reader to process billions of dollars of transactions.

HOW TO LAND A JOB IN ELECTRONICS DESIGN

There are several career paths for students interested in electronics design. Jobs in electronics design include electrical and electronic engineers, electrical and electronic engineering technicians, and software engineers. Regardless of specific career path, high school students interested in electronics design can take classes in physics, algebra, trigonometry, and calculus to prepare for a career in this field. In addition, classes in drafting can help a student learn skills that will be needed to prepare technical drawings. In a makerspace, students can take classes and gain hands-on experience working with electronic components and circuits.

Many people interested in electronics design earn a bachelor's degree in electrical engineering, electronics engineering, or a related field from a four-year college or university. In these programs, students will take classes in math, science, computer science, and engineering. They will study areas such as digital systems design, differential equations, electrical circuits, microprocessors, and more. Many electrical and electronics engineers also take computer programming courses as part of their electrical engineering program. Many bachelor's degree programs include classroom lectures along with hands-on laboratory work and fieldwork, where students design and test electronic devices and systems. Some colleges offer cooperative programs, which are a type of internship that allows students to combine classroom study with practical, hands-on work experience with professionals in their field.

For students who want to become electrical and electronics engineering technicians, an associate's degree in electrical or electronics engineering technology is common. Students can enroll in a two-year program at technical schools or local community colleges. In these programs, students will take courses in programming languages, chemistry, physics, logical processors, circuits, and more.

For some positions, electrical and electronics engineers earn advanced degrees. Some universities offer five-year programs in which a student can earn a bachelor's degree and a master's degree. Master's degrees and PhDs are typically required for teaching positions at colleges and universities as well as for some positions in research and development labs.

HANDS-ON ELECTRONICS

At New Jersey's New Milford High School, students can explore electronics in a makerspace in the school's library. In activities with simulated circuits, students get hands-on experiences with series and parallel circuits that allow them to experience power sources, current flow, and activation of elements such as buzzers, motors, and lights. Students are also able to explore current flows through light bulbs in circuits powered by batteries and controlled by switches. Library media specialist Laura Fleming described the students' work in a 2014 case study on the littleBits blog:

> Once in the Makerspace, students began to create, tinker, and invent to learn concepts related to circuitry. When they made littleBits circuits that rotated paper hands and another that created light up shoes, they overcame initial impediments and experienced success. They had to troubleshoot to find a broken lead on a connection to the battery or find an open circuit because a connection that appeared to be made was electrically disconnected.

According to Fleming, the hands-on experiences in the makerspace helped reinforce classroom learning with the students and sparked curiosity in them. She said in the case study:

> Many of our students have taken it upon themselves to spend their nights and weekends continuing to learn about concepts they were introduced to in our makerspace, and then have come into the school excited about this learning and eager to share it with me, their teachers and their peers.

While licensing is not required for most entry-level positions, some employers may require candidates for more advanced positions to be licensed. To earn a Professional Engineering (PE) license, engineers must graduate from a program that is accredited by the Accreditation Board for Engineering and Technology, Inc. (ABET), have several years of work experience, and pass at least two exams. Once they have earned a PE license, electrical engineers can supervise other engineers, sign off on projects, and contract directly with the public to provide services. Electrical and electronics engineers can also earn certifications that show technical expertise in specialized areas. While not always required, earning a license or certification can improve a person's chances of landing a job or promotion.

Because technology changes quickly, it is essential for electronics designers to stay current and informed on the latest developments in their field. They can do this by reading industry publications, enrolling in courses, and attending conferences. Many states require licensed engineers to take continuing education courses to keep their license current.

JOB OUTLOOK

According to the Bureau of Labor Statistics, jobs for electrical and electronics engineers, which includes electronics designers, are projected to grow 7 percent from 2016 to 2026. Employment of electrical and electronics engineering technicians is also projected to grow 2 percent over the same ten-year period. While employment for electronic

An engineer measures voltage on a conductor board in a maker-space workshop as she works on developing a component for a new electronics product.

engineers and technicians is expected to slow in manufacturing organizations, most opportunities for professionals in this field will occur in engineering services firms. As organizations try to reduce expenses, many will turn to contracting with engineering services firms instead of hiring their own full-time engineering staff. Engineers working for engineering services firms will be needed to develop sophisticated consumer electronics products.

Electrical and electronics engineers will also be needed in research and development. As technology continues to evolve at a rapid pace, experienced engineers will be needed to develop new technologies, systems, and devices. These engineers will be important for the development of cutting-edge semiconductors, communications technologies, and solar arrays. They will also be needed to work on electronic devices and components increasingly being included in cars, household appliances, and other household electronics systems.

Although competition for jobs will be strong, electrical and electronics engineers with an engineering degree from an ABET-accredited program, advanced degrees, and related work experience will have the best job prospects.

CHAPTER FIVE

DESIGNER FINE ART AND CRAFTS

Scottish artist and designer James Abell creates three-dimensional art that combines 3D graphics, 3D printing, and traditional drawing. In the last few years, he has completed three artist-in-residence periods with makerspaces—EchoFab in Montreal and FabLabs in London and Iceland. Abell's time in art residencies at makerspaces have made him an advocate of the maker movement and makerspaces. On his website, he explains how having access to makerspaces impacted his art:

> During a long stay in Canada in 2015, I got an arts residency in EchoFab Montreal. I was like a kid in a candy store, I could use 3D printers, laser cutters to work this technology into my traditional drawing line energy work. The "lightbulb" switched on. From there, I also got art residencies at FabLab London and also FabLab Isafjordur in Iceland. These

In St. Petersburg, Russia, people gather at the Fab Lab Polytech area during PolyFest, the largest university festival of scientific achievements in Europe.

residencies enabled me to master the latest machines such as 3D printers, laser cutters etc, while at the same time using traditional art methods such as drawing and also my 3D graphics skills.

CREATING WORKS OF ART

Designer craftspeople and fine artists work with a variety of materials and techniques to create art that they can sell and exhibit. Craft art is a type of art that typically involves the creation of handmade goods that are both attractive and useful. Craft artists work with many different types of materials and techniques to create functional, handmade objects such as furniture, ceramics, pottery, textiles, glassware, jewelry, and more. Some artists work with wood to create unique objects such as bird houses, furniture, and woven baskets. Textile artists weave, knit, crochet, or sew textiles to create handcrafted materials, blankets, clothing, and handbags. Ceramic artists use clay to shape, form, and mold objects, while glass artists work with glass, blowing, shaping, or joining it to create objects. Other craft artists use metals, stones, beads, and other materials to create beautiful pieces of jewelry.

Fine artists such as painters, sculptors, and illustrators create art that is meant to be looked at and enjoyed, rather than used as a functional object. These artists often try to communicate ideas or feelings through their art. Fine-art painters paint a variety of scenes and styles and use different materials, such as watercolors, oil paints, or acrylic paints. Sculptors create 3D pieces of art, often molding and joining materials such as clay, glass, plastic, and metals. Fine artists typically display their work in museums, art galleries, or at craft fairs. Fine art can also be displayed in corporate offices or in private homes. Sometimes, an artist will create a piece of art for a specific client, at his or her request. Most of the time, however, an artist will sell artwork through art galleries or dealers.

CREATING ART IN A MAKERSPACE

Aliza Vaida is a sculptor, painter, and artist who often creates at the Artisan's Asylum, a makerspace in Somerville, Massachusetts. Vaida cannot remember a time when she was not drawing or sculpting something. She graduated from Boston University with a degree in painting and sculpture and currently works as a custom framer. She first learned about Artisan's Asylum from a friend and decided to join the makerspace because it gave her access to the tools she needed to work on her art.

Hundreds of makerspace enthusiasts gather at a Massachusetts makerspace conference where they listen to panelist discussions and work in small groups to build creations.

At the makerspace, Vaida works mostly with wood to create wood furniture and creates large metal sculptures out of found materials. In an interview on the Artisan's Asylum website, she described her passion for art, "I have always loved creating things and I particularly love transforming found objects into beautiful pieces of art." She also talked about how the makerspace has helped her art, "I have been able to use a full wood shop and metal shop that would have been impossible for me to afford otherwise. Also the community here has been invaluable. With any questions I have had to complete a project there has been someone to help."

HOW TO BECOME A FINE OR CRAFT ARTIST

There are no specific educational requirements for a career in fine or craft art. Craft artists often do not need to have a formal degree, however, to be successful, they must be very skilled. To improve their skills, many craft artists take classes and workshops to improve their skills and crafting techniques. Students in high school who are interested in becoming craft artists should take classes in art, shop, and home economics to learn some of the basic skills they will need, such as drawing, woodworking and metalworking, and sewing. Many of these skills can also be developed through classes and workshops offered at a makerspace.

Many fine artists choose to pursue a formal degree, such as a bachelor of arts (BA) or a bachelor of fine arts (BFA) from a four-year college or university, that gives them

INTRICATE CARVING

Ben Satterfield is a talented designer and CNC operator—a computer numerically controlled machine specialist, or someone who operates a piece of equipment that is run by computer programming—who works out of the Idea Foundry, a makerspace in Columbus, Ohio. He uses his skills to create modern designs in traditional wood materials. In one recent project, Satterfield was hired by a client to create a replacement for a large, decorative wood carving that had deteriorated beyond repair over the years. The client challenged Satterfield to create a design that would be traditional enough to fit the look of the one-hundred-year-old house, but also have a modern twist. Satterfield took the client's wish for a modern floral design and incorporated it into traditional wood materials. "I started by tracing the images she gave me to get a 2D drawing that I used to make a 3D model of the flower using Vectric's Aspire software. I then used the Shopbot CNC router here at the Foundry to carve out the piece which took almost 8 hours," he said in a profile on the Idea Foundry website. Satterfield completed the piece by sanding, texturing, and staining it to give it a rustic, antique look.

the opportunity to improve their artistic skills. Formal training can benefit students by giving them the opportunity to explore new techniques, materials, and methods. These programs allow students to take classes in studio art and art history, along with basic core classes in English, marketing, social sciences, and natural sciences. Some students pursue training at an independent art and design school, where they can earn a certificate in an art field, or an associate's, bachelor's, or master's degree in fine arts. In these programs, students work on their artistic skills by taking classes in drawing, painting, pottery, sculpture, woodworking, and more.

In all educational programs, artists have the opportunity to develop their portfolio. A portfolio is a collection of the artist's work, which shows his or her talent, creativity, and style. Having a good art portfolio is essential to landing a job in the field. Prospective employers look at an artist's portfolio when deciding whether or not to hire him or her

In a woodworking workshop in a makerspace, a carpenter uses a variety of tools to carve a wooden horse sculpture.

or buy his or her work. An art portfolio can be physical, online, or a combination of the two.

JOB OUTLOOK

Overall, the outlook for those pursuing craft and fine-artist careers is good. According to the Bureau of Labor Statistics, employment of craft and fine artists is projected to grow 6 percent from 2016 to 2026. This rate of growth is about the average growth rate for all occupations.

The job outlook for craft and fine artists depends primarily on the overall economy. Most people spend money on art only if they have enough left after paying necessity expenses, such as rent, food, health care, and transportation. When the economy is good, people have more money to spend on art. During an economic downturn, people generally spend less money on art. However, a growing interest in the United States in buying locally made products and handcrafted goods is expected to drive demand for craft and fine artists.

Competition for jobs in this career field is strong, as there are often more qualified artists than available jobs. Many artists choose to work independently and are self-employed. Many sell their work in the same online marketplaces, which increases competition. In addition, competition to have an artist's work shown in an art gallery will be strong because of limited gallery space. Because the demand for artwork can fluctuate significantly, many artists find that they need to supplement their income from their fine art and crafts with another job or source of income. Some work as art directors, curators, or at other jobs in museums or art galleries. Others teach craft or art classes or hold workshops in schools or studios.

Despite the intense competition in this field, many art galleries, studios, and buyers are looking to discover artists with talent and style. Artists who have mastered their skills and techniques and have learned how to market themselves and their work are likely to have the most success in this career field.

CHAPTER SIX

FINDING A JOB IN DESIGN AND PROTOTYPING

C hoosing the right career can seem overwhelming. There are so many options, finding the right one can seem impossible. Yet with a little planning and preparation, discovering a satisfying career and landing a job in design and prototyping is possible.

ASSESS YOUR SKILLS AND MAKE A PLAN

One of the first steps in preparing for a career in any field, including design and prototyping, is doing a skills assessment. A skills assessment asks a lot of questions and forces students to think about what they are good at and what they like to do. Typical questions include:

What do you enjoy doing?
What ideas and beliefs are important to you at work?

College students attend a job fair where they gather information about open jobs, companies, and the business cards of hiring managers.

What is your personality like?
Do you have a natural talent for something—like math or art?
What skills do you have?
What type of location do you want to work in—indoor or outdoor, office or factory?
Are there any special circumstances that might limit what career you can do?

Using this information, students can explore careers. They can go online to research different careers and job descriptions, learn about specific job duties, salary information, and job outlooks. With this research, students can narrow their focus on the careers that most interest them. They may want to talk to someone who is working in these careers to see what the day-to-day job is like. Once students have completed their research, they can decide which career is the best fit for them.

Next, students should plan how they will prepare for their chosen career. What skills and training do people working in this career have? What preparation, education, and training are needed to be successful? With this information, students can create a career plan that identifies the steps to land a job in the chosen career. The plan should include short-term and long-term goals. For example, a person who wants to be a CAD designer may have a short-term goal of learning how to use a new CAD program and a long-term goal of creating a 3D-printed prototype from a CAD design that can be shown to prospective employers in a portfolio.

TARGETING COMPANIES AND FINDING OPEN JOBS

A great job rarely falls into a person's lap unexpectedly. Instead, people who are actively looking for a job in design and prototyping can get a step ahead of the competition by identifying and targeting companies where they would like to work. To identify target companies, a person can review lists of the top companies to work for or visit the local chamber of

A student researches companies and job descriptions and identifies potential employers as part of her job search.

commerce to get a listing of local companies. Professional associations in design and prototyping can also be great resources for identifying companies in a particular field or industry. To research these companies, job seekers can go online. Company websites and sites such as LinkedIn and Glassdoor have information about companies, including employee reviews, company statistics, open positions, ratings, and more.

Once a person has identified potential employers, he or she can start searching for open positions. Many companies have a page on their website that lists open job opportunities. On this page, job seekers can find information such as job descriptions, requirements, and how to apply. In some cases, applicants may even be able to apply for the job online. Job seekers can also use job search engines to search by company name to find additional open job postings. Having a contact at a target company can help give a candidate an opening to learn about open positions and get his or her résumé in front of the right person.

WRITING A RÉSUMÉ

Whether applying for a job in person or online, applicants need to have a strong résumé that highlights their unique skills and experiences. A résumé presents an applicant's employment history, educational background, skills, and qualifications. An applicant's résumé should also present information specific to the jobs for which he or she is applying and show why he or she would be a good fit for the position and company. While a great résumé will not land an applicant a job by itself, it can get someone in the door for an interview.

While it might seem intimidating, writing a great résumé is a simple step-by-step process. Before beginning, applicants should ask themselves some questions that will shape their résumé. Are they looking for an entry-level job? Are they changing careers or returning to the workforce after a long time off? Answering these questions can help an applicant better understand their objectives and guide their résumé writing.

Every résumé requires several basic elements. A résumé should include all relevant educational degrees or certifications. It should also highlight any relevant work and volunteer experience. With each position, applicants should focus on achievements, especially those that relate to the job for which they are applying. A résumé must include an applicant's contact information—his or her full name, email address, and phone number. Many design professionals also include one or more skills sections on their résumés that lists specific programming languages, software tools, art and modeling skills, and more. To get inspiration on what to include and how to format a résumé, applicants can search online for examples of résumés in their field, industry, or company.

In addition to a résumé, applicants will also need to write a cover letter. A cover letter can be mailed or included in the body of an email or as an email attachment. Applicants should check to see which method a potential employer prefers and follow it. A cover letter highlights the applicant's accomplishments and convinces the hiring manager to read the applicant's résumé and schedule an

THE IMPORTANCE OF NETWORKING

Networking can help a person find a job and get hired. Networking involves using personal, professional, and school contacts to help in a job search or give career advice. Networking contacts can help applicants learn more about design and prototyping, get career advice, learn about job opportunities, or get an "in" at a desired company. Networking contacts can also review an applicant's résumé or portfolio. Rob Bye is a cofounder of the product design consultancy Morrama and believes that networking is an essential part of getting a job in the design industry. In a blog post on the Dezeen website, he said that networking "is pretty important as most people really do get employed through a friend of a friend. Don't simply see it as a way to get a job. Get advice from recent graduates and other professionals on what skills you should improve upon, how to progress as a designer and what sort of fields you should look into. And, crucially, ask them to give feedback on your portfolio."

interview. There are many examples of cover letters on the internet that applicants can review.

PREPARING FOR AN INTERVIEW

Most positions require an in-person interview at which an applicant talks to representatives from the company.

A candidate meets with a hiring manager in a job interview. The candidate has prepared by researching the company and practicing her responses to potential questions.

Applicants can prepare for the interview by researching the company and the employees they will be meeting, reviewing the job description, and practicing their answers to common interview questions such as "Tell me about yourself" and "Why are you interested in this job?" Applicants can also think about examples from their previous work experiences that match skills the employer is looking for. For design jobs, applicants may be asked to describe their design process and to give examples of how they collaborated with a team. Applicants should also prepare a few questions to ask the interviewer that show they are serious about wanting to work in that role.

Interviews for design careers often include portfolio presentations and design challenges. A portfolio presentation gives the interviewer a sense of the applicant's design process and how he or she approaches a design problem. Often, the presentation will include one to two projects. Weston Karnes is a product designer who has been through several product design interviews. He advises applicants to keep it simple and tell a story in their portfolio presentation. He said in a 2017 blog post on Medium.com:

> Presenting a project is simply saying how you got from point A to point B. Regardless of your process, this needs to be communicated. You can touch on specific problems you encountered along the way, branched directions you explored, or other specifics... Regardless of that, the story connecting each part should be communicated. Don't stray far from the core problem(s) and solution.

The interview's design challenge can be either to take home, do on site, or both. Often the challenge is vague, says Karnes, because employers are looking to see how the applicant handles ambiguity and shapes the problem. Karnes recommends that applicants make sure they know what the interviewer wants to see. "You have an hour here at best to compress the whole design process into. Knowing which parts to focus most on, and ultimately, what the interviewer is trying to gauge in your skillset is paramount," he said.

After the interview, applicants should also send a thank-you note to their interviewers to express their appreciation for being given the opportunity to meet with them and to restate their interest in the position. Today, many applicants sent thank-you notes via email.

In today's competitive job market, candidates need to have the knowledge, skills, and experiences to set them apart from other candidates. At makerspaces, those with an interest in careers in design and prototyping can explore and master new skills, techniques, and technologies. These makerspace experiences can help them stand out in a crowded job application pool and land their dream job in design and prototyping.

GLOSSARY

aesthetics How appealing something is to look at.

brainstorm A group discussion that is intended to produce ideas and ways of solving problems.

certification An official document that shows a level of achievement or qualification to work in a certain field.

component A part of a larger whole, especially a part of a machine.

computer-aided design (CAD) The use of computer software to create, modify, and analyze a design.

consumer A person who buys goods and services for personal use.

design requirements The important characteristics that a solution must have in order to be successful.

drafting Technical drawing.

electronics Devices that operate using electrical power.

functionality Being able to serve a purpose well.

industrial design The process of designing goods for mass production.

innovative New and original creativity in thinking.

internship The position of a student or trainee who works in an organization, sometimes without pay, in order to gain work experience.

laser cutter A machine that uses lasers to cut materials.

layout The way in which parts are arranged.

makerspace A creative environment where tools and supplies are provided, allowing makers a space to build and create.

milling A machining process that uses rotating cutters to remove material from a work piece.

prototype A working model of a product.

scale model A copy of an object that is usually smaller than the actual size of the object.

simulations Things that create a virtual environment that looks, feels, and behaves like the real world.

sketch A quick and rough drawing.

tedious Long, slow, and dull.

3D printer A machine that is used to craft a 3D object based on a specific design.

virtual Exists only on a computer, not in the real world.

Artisan's Asylum
10 Tyler Street
Somerville, MA 02143
(617) 284-6878
Website: https://artisansasylum.com/contact
Facebook and Twitter: @ArtisanAsylum
Artisan's Asylum is a makerspace located in Somerville,
    Massachusetts. Its website has a lot of information and
    news about makerspaces, maker profiles, and educa-
    tional programs.

Association of Chartered Industrial Designers in Ontario
    (ACIDO)
998 Bloor Street W.
Bloorcourt PO Box 10508
Toronto, ON M581L0
Canada
Website: http://acido.info
ACIDO is an association of industrial designers in
    Ontario that fosters high standards of design and
    supports designers at all levels of their careers
    through the development and promotion of best prac-
    tices and work opportunities.

Fab Foundation
50 Milk Street, 16th Floor
Boston, MA 02109
(857) 333-7777
Website: http://www.fabfoundation.org
Facebook and Twitter: @FabFndn
Started at MIT, the Fab Foundation is a nonprofit

organization that supports Fab Lab makerspaces around the world.

Industrial Designers Society of America (IDSA)
555 Grove Street, Suite 200
Herndon, VA 20170
(703) 707-6000
Website: http://www.idsa.org
Facebook: @IDSA.org
Twitter: @IDSA
The IDSA is one of the largest industrial design associations, representing thousands of members in the United States and around the world. It promotes and educates about industrial design.

Make:
1700 Montgomery Street, Suite 240
San Francisco, CA 94111
Website: https://makershare.com
Facebook: @makemagazine
Twitter: @make
Make: is a global platform that provides opportunities for makers to come together to learn, share, make, and collaborate. Its website offers information about the latest maker news and profiles as well as upcoming Maker Faires around the country.

MakerWiz
10909 Yonge Street, Unit 211
Richmond Hill, ON L4C 3E3
Canada
(289) 637-1333

Website: https://makerwiz.com
Facebook and Twitter: @makerwiz
Founded in 2014, Makerwiz is dedicated to promoting
    the maker movement by promoting the knowledge
    and application of emerging educational technol-
    ogies, such as 3D printing, drone robotics, and
    wearable electronics, and empowering a new genera-
    tion of makers and inventors.

Product Development and Management Association (PDMA)
1000 Westgate Drive, Suite 252
St. Paul, MN 55114
(651) 290-6280
Website: http://www.pdma.org
Facebook and Twitter: @PDMAIntl
The PDMA is a global association that includes product
    development and management professionals from a
    variety of industries. The organization's website offers
    information about the latest industry news, conferences,
    and certification opportunities.

ThingTank Lab
376 Bathurst Street
Toronto, ON M5T 2S6
Canada
Website: http://www.criticalmaking.com/ddimit
Twitter: @thingtankTO
The ThingTank Lab is an open, community-based collabora-
    tive ideation lab where the exploration, experimentation,
    and exchange of ideas are developed toward the build-
    ing of internet-enabled "things."

FOR FURTHER READING

Arato, Rona. *Design It! The Ordinary Things We Use Every Day and the Not-So-Ordinary Ways They Came to Be.* Toronto, Canada: Tundra Books, 2010.

Challoner, Jack. *Maker Lab: 28 Super Cool Projects: Build * Invent * Create * Discover.* New York, NY: DK Publishing, 2016.

Fiell, Charlotte, and Peter Fiell. *Industrial Design: A–Z.* Los Angeles, CA: TASCHEN, 2016.

Fiell, Charlotte, and Peter Fiell. *The Story of Design from the Paleolithic to the Present.* New York, NY: The Monacelli Press, 2016.

Graves, Aaron, and Colleen Graves. *20 Makey Makey Projects for the Evil Genius.* New York, NY: McGraw-Hill Education, 2017.

Graves, Colleen, and Aaron Graves. *The Big Book of Maker-space Projects: Inspiring Makers to Experiment, Create, and Learn.* New York, NY: McGraw-Hill Education, 2016.

Heitkamp, Kristina Lyn. *Creating with Digital Sewing Machines (Getting Creative with Fab Lab).* New York, NY: Rosen Central, 2017.

Kamberg, Mary-Lane. *Creating with Laser Cutters and Engravers (Getting Creative with Fab Lab).* New York, NY: Rosen Central, 2017.

Lees-Maffei, Grace. *Iconic Design: 50 Stories about 50 Things.* New York, NY: Bloomsbury, 2014.

Pieri, Jules, and Joanne Domeniconi. *Makers Who Made It: 100 Stories of Starting a Business.* Cambridge, MA: The Grommet, 2016.

Porterfield, Jason. *Creating with Milling Machines (Getting Creative with Fab Lab).* New York, NY: Rosen Central, 2017.

BIBLIOGRAPHY

Artisan's Asylum. "Aliza Vaida—Sculptor, Painter, Artist." Retrieved September 15, 2018. https://artisansasylum .com/ourmembers.

Bye, Rob. "Dezeen Jobs: How to Get Your First Design Job." Dezeen.com, October 23, 2015. https://www .dezeen.com/2015/10/23 /advice-rob-bye-dezeen-jobs-design-graduates.

Coyle, Kathleen. "Meet James Abell: 3D Artist and Designer." 3D Printing Chat, July 11, 2017. http:// chat3d.co.uk/meet-james-abell-3d-artist-designer.

Cummings, Mike. "A Maker Space Where Art and Technology Merge." Yale University, February 8, 2018. https:// news.yale.edu/2018/02/08 /maker-space-where-art-and-technology-merge.

Design Tech CAD Academy. "Introduction to CAD." Retrieved September 15, 2018. https://www .designtechcadacademy.com/knowledge-base /introduction-to-cad.

Displayplan. "Day in the Life of a Tech Designer." Retrieved September 15, 2018. http://www.displayplan.com /news/2017/day-life-tech-designer.

Doyle, Alison. "How to Build a Resume in 7 Easy Steps," The Balance Careers, August 6, 2018. https://www .thebalancecareers.com /easy-steps-to-build-a-resume-4122296.

Gosalvez, Emma. "Engineering Students Explore Prototyping Through Maker Opportunities at Behrend." Penn State.com, May 2, 2018. https://news.psu.edu /story/519738/2018/05/02

/academics/engineering-students-explore
-prototyping-through-maker.

Idea Foundry. "The Art of CNC." February 21, 2018.
https://ideafoundry.com/blog/art-cnc.

Indeed Career Guide. "6 Universal Rules for Resume Writing." Retrieved September 15, 2018. https://www
.indeed.com/career-advice/resumes-cover-letters/6
-universal-rules-for-resume-writing.

Inertia. "The Three Phases of Product Prototyping."
Retrieved September 12, 2018. https://
inertiaengineering.com/three-phases-prototyping.

James Abell Art. Retrieved September 20, 2018. http://
www.jamesabellart.com/about-james-abell-art.

Jobsite. "What Does a Product Designer Do? The Life of a
Dyson Designer." March 2, 2018. https://www.jobsite
.co.uk/worklife/what-does-a-product-designer-do-the
-life-of-a-dyson-designer-24461.

Kalish, Jon. "High-Tech Maker Spaces: Helping Little Start-
ups Make It Big." NPR.org, April 30, 2014. https://www
.npr.org/sections
/alltechconsidered/2014/04/30/306235442/high
-tech-maker-spaces-helping-little-startups-make-it-big.

Karnes, Weston. "Learnings from Product Design Interviews." Medium.com, October 3, 2017. https://
medium.com/@westonkarnes/learnings-from
-product-design-interviews-7a494d531960.

Lapowsky, Issie. "Jack Dorsey: The Man Who Made the
Cash Register Obsolete." Inc.com. Retrieved September
12, 2018. https://www.inc.com/audacious-companies
/issie-lapowsky/square.html.

McKay, Dawn Rosenberg. "The Career Planning Process."

The Balance Careers, December 21, 2017. https://
www.thebalancecareers.com
/the-career-planning-process-524774.

Pieri, Jules, and Joanne Domeniconi. *Makers Who Made It: 100 Stories of Starting a Business*. Cambridge, MA: The Grommet, 2016.

Rivlin, Gary. "Chain of DIY Stores Sparks Inventions." *Newsweek*, June 26, 2011. https://www.newsweek.com/chain-diy-stores-sparks-inventions-68019.

TargetJobs. "Electronic Engineering: Industry Sector Overview." Retrieved September 15, 2018. https://targetjobs.co.uk/career-sectors/engineering/advice/282433-electronic-engineering-industry-sector-overview.

INDEX

ABOUT THE AUTHOR

Carla Mooney is a graduate of the University of Pennsylvania. Before becoming an author, she spent several years working in finance as an accountant. Today, she writes for young people and is the author of many books for young adults and children. Mooney enjoys learning new skills and plans to visit a makerspace in the near future.

PHOTO CREDITS